PLANT DADDY

PLANT DADDY

by
Renée Rigdon

Accents Publishing • Lexington, Kentucky • 2025

Printed in the United States of America

Accents Publishing
Editor: Katerina Stoykova
Cover Image: *Wols Dans le sable (enlisé, une seule main surgit)* by Wols

Library of Congress Control Number: 2025931828
ISBN: 978-1-961127-13-5
First Edition

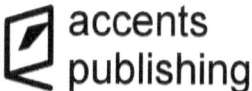

Accents Publishing is an independent press for brilliant voices. For a catalog of current and upcoming titles, please visit us on the Web at

www.accents-publishing.com

CONTENTS

the gleaning

For my dad, who taught me how to change a tire, to make sure the hose wasn't attached when the freeze comes, to watch out for deer on the highway, and the importance of a good roll of duct tape. Every one of these actions was an act of love, even if I didn't always recognize it at the time. His presence on this earth was a net positive.

Larry Wayne Butler
1954-2024

the air

Even if I knew that tomorrow the world would go to pieces, I would still plant my apple tree.

—Martin Luther

BRIGHT, INDIRECT LIGHT

You have every right to this perfect, sunny spot.
Decked decadent in
warm soil and nutrient and
moisture measurements met.

Here, on this quiet sill,
light spills—gentle
through each verdant velvet tendril—some
as
long
as
a lifetime—some snipped short
to save you from that

which was done or
undone or
never done but should have been and even so

You are still so completely intact.
You are still here.

You are sacred and you are seen.

You are safe.

THOUGHTS &

Prayers are fragile things.
    Best met by perfect pitch and
    slope from the sunny window
    slaked by rainwater, sacred and wild-caught

answered wrong, a prayer withers into loose fists.
    Lost.

Prayers are best fed by freedom.
    In 2023, there were more than 350 pieces of legislation that have
    asked of me to never exist.
They prefer I would be what they think I am.
    To return to smallness.
    Prune back this new growth that I know
                is mine.

and if I died out, they'd be fine with that, too.

Please don't take this from me.
    I cherish this version of myself that splays open their
    palms to the morning light, red-veined and plaintive. Full.

Prayers are fragile things, and I am not so prayerful
    to think I am enough. I am not
    a fighter.

I am bluster and bravado.
I am trying to believe that I can help anyone—anything
    survive
        this.

I am curled into loose fists, held high, begging not
    to use them.

Pleading for a gentler kind of rain.

FOR THE CONSERVATORY

"I never once lost a plant,"

I am a liar and I am
building this (green)house of cards
aside philodendron and
      peperomia and
      pilea peperomioides
so the shop clerk will approve of me.

I don't want them to think
    that I could ever fail at tending to the susurrant
    respiration of my loves I …

let that lie
    <u>There</u>
just beside his ashes, brought home
in a generic white box that refuses to be complicit in my plans.

—back at the shop—
We are together
holding a resplendent dieffenbachia
"this one is 'dumb cane,'" they tell me, "put it in your mouth &
your tongue will swell you speechless."
I stroke its prideful leaves and imagine the secrets we will

    keep

the seeds

Life is a progress, and not a station.

—Ralph Waldo Emerson

Plants want to grow; they are on your side as long as you are reasonably sensible.

—Anne Wareham

&THE SUNLIGHT, THROUGH HER LEAVES—

If you ask me what kind of animal I want to be, I will say,
"plant"

every time—I mean
    occasionally—I mean
        if I answer the question at all.

I want to dig my toes so deep into the soil
    that they form roots and talk to the worms.

Also known as, *ew, that's weird*
        you're not playing the game right
        get it together

This one has it all the way together.

Her throne is a pot
on a windowsill in a spot
that she picked, not

                me.

She sits on her splay of tangled moss in radiant contemplation.

Her roots grow and crackle and cackle at the jokes the dirt knows
She does not spend a
second
    worried that her disarray does anything less than multiply
Beauty & Value.

She's a shining one, Messy Bitch—
I mean Vanessa—
I mean, *Haworthia cymbiformis*

    AKA, Cathedral Window
    also known as a portal—an aperture—*la finestra*

in the tower or edifice or hall of my
succulent transformation

She doesn't care to be called Vanessa.
She does not worry—the way I do—that her true name is too
profane.
She knows it's all sacred.

The chaos. The moss. The light.

When you ask her what type of animal she would be, you can very
nearly hear the sigh.
Just out of
     reach.
It says,
"if you could be

Me,

          why the fuck would you be any
          body
                    else?"

ABOUT THE SPIDER PLANT

the unnamed one, I mean
The Unnamed One,
I mean, *Chlorophytum comosum*

    AKA Spider plant
    also known as arachnid, tarantula, wanderer

being … posed,
positioned, just so,
    to know in the flow of their mane of spiderlet
        and tendrils
        and bottomless grace

Great
—and terrible—
things

If you ask The Unnamed One what kind of animal They want to be,
you will feel the faint tickle at the nape of your neck.

A breath weighted feral with
a predator's
        hush.

They know there is power in the naming of things. Of displacing the
Norm
    of such thoughtless disclosure.

Only The Fool goes
where everybody knows their name.

No. They keep Their own counsel.

If you ask me what kind or animal I want to be, I might end up giving
you
my social security number.

I am not great at many games.

The Unnamed One hears, waits, protects.
    Witnesses.
And does not waste Their precious
time with dallies such as these.

But Every Last One Wants

to be known
—a bit.

so in that dark mystery,
the almost just there,
    <a roar a rumble just beneath the canopy>

        —a lion—

GLOWING

Vibrant and bitter-lemon-green
piling and unfurling, Hearts
at the end of his sleeves
fall
around his handmade Roy G. Biv pot
that began its life somewhere
in Portugal.

He is our own pot of gold at the end of the rainbow

Glenn,
　　　　AKA "Low drama Glenn," I mean
Philodendron Cordatum
Also known as Neon Philodendron

A blazing, radiant, shining boi

And Born and planted to yearn.
So silent at first, then unlearning to keep
—quiet—

He gets two or three new leaves a week,
you know
Now that he's let everyone know exactly what he needs.

these victories are so rare

and never less

than hard-won

If you ask Glenn what kind of animal he wants to be, he'll tell you
—he's the only one who tells you true
—I'm so used to lies,

but here, the honest truth.
"A firefly. Lit up. Undeniable."

Glenn has never heard the *fado*.
to pine, to covet, to yearn, to ache

but he feels it

How brave must it be, he thinks, to look fate in the eye and say,

"Your eyes are mine, because with your beauty, you've left me blind."

PIZZA, MY HEART

Penny Pepperoni, I mean Pink Lady, I mean *peperomia caperata*

AKA my best girl

also known as the growing, breathing heart-stone
of the hab

The thing about peperomias is they can live through anything, except
too much attention.

I have been overwatering my insecurities and my plants

—to believe I have control—

—to convince myself that care is care, always—
now Penny's wilted over on the dining table, asking for more and
less than my insistent incantations to

"come back"

If you ask Penny Pepperoni what kind of animal she wants to be, you
will remember your front yard, you, rolled up like a snack wrap in a
bright

yellow

quilt,
so that the earth could hold you as safe as your great grandmother's
hands

Penny Pepperoni plays the game exactly right.

If you ask me eighty times what kind of animal I would be, I'd say,
"Plant,"

Every
time.

Except this one. This time, and only this,

the words dripping deep
sublingual
down into my ragged throat

I am not ready.

—please—
—be the one that can help—

STAY GOLD

Xe is an exuberance of
vine and leaf and node and green and
      reach

Golden Pothos, or
Xyr Unspeakable Lightness, one Rue ThaDay
Long may Xe reign

Xe knows what it is to
     grasp
to carry
the holy dapple of noonlight through the canopy forest
so far from home that
the rain is not but
half-remembered and poorly-brought by
The Grieving Widow,
they are forgiven. Of course they are forgiven. They are, always for
Rue knows only magnanimity,
       inimitably.
Xe is no stranger to wilt and pestilence and time.
To not
Enough
Light

Xe understands what The Widow cannot.
Yet.
   cannot yet.
cannot yet realize that since they are holding these:
   a quasar
   a star

Impossible Tragedy and Unbearable Transcendence
   in just

one
hand.

That The other is left free, outstretched west toward the sun.

.

HELLO

      You are in that vacuum-sealed space between who
      You are &
who you thought *you wanted you* to
         be—airless and adhesed
         by dreams you want you *to want to*
         have.

—you deserve so much more than your heart gives permission to ask—

FROM HERE

      I want to tell you—and cannot—
        that I have nothing to say that couldn't be said better by
  a countless thrashing stream of motivational posters,

  of neon-dyed gerbera bouquets with smiling crinkly wrappers

  of Dove bar foils, smoothed and worried and later, trashed
  like we do with Prayers

      What I am saying is I am the basic bitch of meme-able life
      advice

      What I am saying is
I am wrapped

      around your jagged pieces with my own shards bound down
      against

      my shredding chest with (Nascar-approved)
      duct tape.

      What I am saying is
I am trying so hard to hold you together
      And if I fail, remember.

TO WHEREVER THIS HAS TAKEN YOU

Remember?
We laughed so hard sometimes that the universe forgot itself and cracked a smile.

the dirt

Each one desires to be a flower, but none wants to be a leaf.

—Leo Patrick Lipana

I keep turning over new leaves, and spoiling them, as I used to spoil my copybooks; and I make so many beginnings there never will be an end.

—Louisa May Alcott

HELIOTROPIC, OR "AND HE START TO RUNNIN' WITH THE CHURCH MONEY AND THE LADY AT 911 SAID, 'DON'T YOU CHASE HIM' AND I SAID, 'OH, I'M CHASIN' HIM'."

Here, deep rooted in our after noon, we turn

> Like poppies chasing the high of the sun
> Like hungry children to a porch light.
> Like cat hair to this inherited sweater, you
>   promised to keep pristine.

to attend to this radiant hero's yarn:

"Y'all ain't gonna believe this."

CLOUD WATCHING

Our little bodies were guarded,
sun-warmed and defended.
At watch on the boundaries of the blanket on the lawn
butter-yellow and threadworn cloak of becoming
    Right here, an impossibility of clouds
    Right here, pulled in by the tide of our wishes
    from the tousled heads of dandelions.

This one looks like a ship.
This one looks like a dog.
That one looks like a memory—

    Our foreheads, pressed together
    Sticky and giggling
    Dissolved by distance, each
    Staring straight into one Cyclops eye,
    Making us something fierce enough to survive the oncoming storm

"It's so much harder to be grown," the oracle intones
And we forget the transient powerlessness of being
        Children

So many decades—epics—away, I am
    Right here
            So close
if I stretch out a lotus-fuzzed tongue I could take
a fibrous swipe of this cloud and feel that spun memory
    dissolve,
briny and petrichor on my breath.

So close that it could rest its misted forehead gently onto mine,
my unrelenting heat and its ever-distant cool a
    rumble

"I remember this one," it would say, a squint at the monster
I've become, all admiration and no fear,
"This one looks like thunder."

GRANDMOTHER-LAND

> "I didn't realize. All that was going on in life and we never noticed.
> Take me back."
>
> —Thornton Wilder, *Our Town*

It's a taut wind
        up this
    forest
ridge

It would be a squint of sunlight, grace, and Heaven
Hill to grant me this pass as safe
 for two
    cross-wending
        bodies in motion
                        bent
scraped inclose to an eversteep and
                        imminent down
                                fall

    I am without
        weight and I am halfway
        between floating, halfway
        between falling through

beautiful / golden / motes
            down
        this ancient mountainside

Guided and Guarded
        you drive us
along the hazy graveled edge.
        I am so
                held by this moment
Safe & Sure of that safety and
    right

in these woods, dense with vine and mystery
& awe

I won't know yet, then
that in less than three years
            you'll stop knowing how to be my dad.

And I'll never know why
I'll never know why and anyway

My memory will be thick and slow with years of kick-
      ing the tires to prove its still good despite the trespasses—theirs—
      and the cheap booze—mine—

gone but not forgotten

I don't know yet that I'll be ever-searching and
not know how to find this forest pass … still

I will miss believing someone's steady hands were on the wheel.
That someone knew where we were going
That someone knew how we were going to make it
                                    home.

ATLAS

Every bleary morning we can remember

We snip gently away those rosebush thorns of last night's
dreams wrapped tight-not-tight
around the rusted cage of our ribs.

From here we lean so close to the mirror
near enough for our vigilant
and myopic eyes,
for tired and tinning ears
breath held to witness stillness between each shaking,
careful
clip

We cannot remove every sticking vine and save still
this flowering body.

There is math in the gardening.
How many more nights can we cut away before we can't?

But still. For now.
beneath the shear noise and falling,
wasted vegetation, we find

the path marked, faded:

"This
        is where this is going."

DEEP ROUTES

Growth is only part of it, in this search to
stop.

—recalculating—
the path to that person you thought you might be.

Did we learn that moss does not care about north or south, but thrives
on moist surfaces? That

our first glances in lost woods are just clickbait distractions
that keep us in the weeds? that
stop.

—recalculating—
handsy brambles have copped their share of scratches—
    shallow
and gouges?
    so many

Please
    imagine at the way the light hits the trees.
    Find the ways water fell to its knees.
    Becomes soft lichen altars not
    unlike relics.

        These are familiar temples whose steps you've kissed a million
        times before.

Look again.
    If life should have to fight so
    just to cling tight to
    these cragging surfaces

Hallowed & Hard.
    (It doesn't have to be so hard, does it?)

But look away. Then,
you'll know,
if you've found your north.

TRAILHEAD OF A PARALLEL WORLD

In some universe, somewhere
we can be anything.

So I am a path through these woods
&You,
    you are the signs marked
    into that path

We are guiding the hikers
    and the travelers
    the families and the loners
                together
    the sunlight dances across our features
      warm

No one is lost.
No one is ever lost.

GOOD VIBES

Listen

    press your ear left
    then right
Into the creeping ivy that overtook everything
       long
before you set foot in this place.

It'll be hard to spin the dial
      low:
bird song & electric hum & your neighbor's questionable taste in men
      but there

just there
—whatever it was that was always going to be—
(that thing you were always going to hear)

    a bark beetle can hear the *pop* of water in the tree roots
    a baby chili can hear the fennel nearby, whispering sweet
        —stay small—
    terrible nothings.

so it grows

    five
    alarm
    hot
before the fennel's song becomes too siren

    to think what you could learn from this moment about playing at
    gods.

The volunteer tomato whispered,
    & whispers still
    "growing only where you're planted is a fool's game"

Gardeners have inexpert & ungentle hands.
It is not your fault.

I AM RECKONING WITH MY INHERITANCE

I must brush away these vines, matted
wilted like tendrils from fevered foreheads
begging to keep burning
just to know my touch

We are delirium-infused and pleading
for deliverance.

I am at war with my ancestors.
Their penchant for neglect
and uneasily allied with their desire to be seen
as "right."

I take these leaves that have curled, desiccated, unthriving.
Grip them tenderly in my hand to edit.
Each crisping, vegetal parchment, a written record
of the ways that I have failed myself.

Am I helping?

Am I making new space for you to flourish?

Or am I telling you in this flickering lamp light,

"I wasn't so bad to you. Look how what's left of you shines."

ONCE UPON

those routes we found—full,
handsy brambles that cropped their share of thin
swift tears across our skin and gouges?
some, but we still thought we were resilient then

                                                    you fell

out of a tree we, jeering, guffawing, goaded you to climb, then
ambled home slow,
far behind the wake of our inside jokes and plans towards
bowls of milk and sugar and the tart bite of wild harvest

Your left toes tender-touched the gravel path,
your bucket of berries abandoned, too hard to balance
your ankle undone

—if we'd resented less the future moldering mess
     would we have carried home your haul?
                                        instead

we left you, our blessings hearty enough to hide
your pain so

We left you.

Was it that day that you learned

the fearful tempo of shame?

What if it all rests on that
one moment?

as thin as a scratch,
portent cast of characters new as a berry
                              green still&
                              on the vine

What if that
is how we taught you that your pain was a burden?
—to us, it was.

There, in our naive summerlight
before your first legit prescription? before
your unintended last?
it goes so fast

—we were not better than this one moment, nor were any of us worse
than our best—

would it have helped to know that?

When we sanctified the folklore of that day, we let your name slip away.
We thought,
to protect you. But

Forgive us.
We were, in that moment, thorns.

but sometimes?
We were Blackberries.
and sometimes still?

a story we stopped telling
because ghost stories aren't paced

for laughs

THE ONE WITH THE COCKROACH

right there, in the bathroom,
I stoop down low with a paper towel.
It's a select-a-size, rose design, diamond texture

a roach, upturned on the tiled floor, dead
    just
    one
not a plague not a sign but beneath her sacred shroud she

    wriggled.

    I smash it—first thing handy—
    a Pyrex measuring cup,
    a sodden wet mash.
    and throw it in the trash

what I'm saying is it wasn't the way I wanted to start my day

    a barefooted death squad. a funeral march
    in lieu of flowers, a bouquet of junk mail and milk rings
    yesterday's banana peels—a slip
                of the tongue
hours later, I will still feel the vibration of
*snap*crunch*twist* and I won't understand yet
    (yet, because I am hopeful)
why

why like
    —a twisted ankle
    —a gritted-teeth "shut up"
    —a broken mason jar, blue, from the woman that named ~~you~~
    me

but
    I don't get to tell you that I saved a bee yesterday

and talked sweetly to a spider
and then whisper, to the mirror

"I am not also this."

A FRIEND SAID ONCE (OF SNAKES)

"You can't trust things without shoulders"
I don't know, but
    the thing that tries to destroy us never answers in a shrug,
    even as it shows you these elbows,
    these hands,

that soft belly—yours—abraded by dirty carpet; dark earth

I wish growing up was so simple as
tearing
    scratching memories against stove corners
        and light switches
        and drawer knobs to loosen flesh and

drop

break off in sheets and fall as fragile fossils to the foresting floor of my
kitchen. I could gather and scatter
them in the yard for crows and small children
—both of whom have shoulders—

They will carry every new knowing home to their kin, and caw,

"Look at how small these once were, just like me."

JUST ONE LAST SUMMER

> We must be willing to get rid of the life we've planned, so as to have
> the life that is waiting for us. The old skin has to be shed before the
> new one can come.
> —Joseph Campbell

This is what it's like to realize,

                    stretching

The pool-damp peel of Mom's last year's bandeau with its swath
of petal pink.
An embarrassment

My growth spurt is making tight obstacles of
my broad shoulders
My not-yet-buds of breasts to be
My hips, just now

                    renouncing

their vernal place, despite the swell of
    this

I am chlorine and
vegetal and
the absence of sunscreen

The hot blush of burn
Lightning and frostbite in the air, exposed
Elemental reminders of each part of me as

                    rushing

I pee, in holy relief.

how strange and hot my insides are against
my pool-wet and
Air-conditioned tenderness

This is not how a girl feels.

In a sudden and momentary relief of
                               meeting
myself. And

I know it, just the way I know this burn will never shuck
Into a base tan and
the pool will turn artifact with algae and
I will pretend that I don't know just how well

this doesn't fit.

TIGHT

The first time They knew *it*
They were peeing.
(Everyone pees).

They wore the hand-me-down swimsuit—a
one-piece undersized for the
wilderness They'd been becoming
for quite
some time now, a fierce rebuttal
of this rootbound vessel.

Shimmy, squeeze, and shuck loose to find
freedom
An exploration of expansion past
cinched shoulders and waist, nipped—
compressing a babe into a birthright

In the tight labyrinth of swimmer's burn vine-traced in pale
tendrils
on Their skin, telling the history of containment in
broiled and buff, there lay at the center,

"I was a boy and they changed me"

A false-bottomed trap of thinking too small and yet
the start
of a truth the only way
They could reckon it
(One turn at a time)

Not real but moreso than
whatever this
Was
This mantle, molded and made-believe
Like it fit.

the sweat

Nothing great is created suddenly, any more than a bunch of grapes or a fig. If you tell me that you desire a fig, I answer you that there must be time. Let it first blossom, then bear fruit, then ripen.

—Epictetus

LONGING: ACT 42, SCENE 6

You are watching this show, set up at the dusty corner
across from your comfort where you were hoping to find
lemonade and instead you got
This

    a middle-age and moldering stage with
    two fading flashlights taped to corners as
    spotlights

    Inside,
Strings fix my hands to this keyboard all
    cardboard and tape
my eyes fix-gazed to the cottonball sky
my jaw pointed to the painted forest
my knees knocked to the scattered earth

I want my wooden organs all Broken and bored through to be
    Blessed
    Released

Remember, as I plead of you this participation:

this show has cost you nothing

There is a latch there, right where anyone would guess it would be
to my heart
Brass and worn, sticking but not stuck.
If no one was looking
(No one is looking)
You might just be able to thumb the catch free.

IF I COULD, I WOULD KISS THEIR SWEET FOREHEADS AND TUCK THEM IN TO TELL THEM—

Bees see me coming a mile away.

There's a tunnel dug in the beam just above
my favorite porch chair.
In the spring, I can't hear my thoughts for the
constant chittering—a click trigger of constant,
low-grade
misophonia.

And sawdust falls in my drink.
Can't have a birch beer for the bees' insistent brooding.

What I'm saying is I've got a problem with my bee hole.

I would give them my everything, yet
At least one a week, seemingly to escape from the delight of warm,
nurturing light,
the wild unjudgement of vines and trees and plentiful pollen …

a bee breaks into my house

She stumbles and fumbles in her personal antigravity towards
Her downfall

I upturn my glass of wet sawdust and roots to
drown the sorrows of my lilies
Pour one out for
the ones I couldn't save
For the ones I've yet to fail in saving

Make a cage, a cloche—a carriage of reprieve
From the ways we can't always be trusted to care
for our selves, I slip
a slim foreclosure notice beneath to hold safe my
Precious cargo

I am so careful but equally inept
—a leg ripped half-off—
—a broken wing—

More than once.

It is a microcosm, a swarm of grief, pollinated
    by every
    tiny
    regret.

I know—as the bees do—what it is to disappear.
    They know—as I do—I am a terrible hero, but a half-decent mom
    —if petty—
—if codependent—
inclined to indulge; desperate to be forgiven.

More live than don't. More forgive than won't.
From their home, a portal no bigger than my pinkie,

they can see this history of my beseeching search,

    How are the bees doing?
    What do carpenter bees like for breakfast?
    Can passion flowers grow here?

A POSTER OF A KITTEN, TAPED JUST ABOVE YOUR KEURIG, REMINDING YOU TO TAKE YOUR MEDS.

Mouth
Command myself, with simple language

to write you this particular poem
to tell you that I have nothing to say that doesn't need to be said
that my significance

holds court
on a throne it made, bespoke
from thrift shop plaques and handknits and the giggly

moments where you laughed at my jokes.
—I am only incorrigible because you keep incorriging me—

Remember?
—it's harder to say, isn't it? these things, if they turn out good?—

this poem is poking your fingers into soft soil and making pockets to
hold seeds that turn into passionflowers—someday
this poem is a hug that squeezes all the broken parts back together into
something that looks almost exactly like the person you were before
this poem is taking your meds and eating a vegetable and getting fresh
air and remembering you are loved
this poem is saying thank you for your presence—not—I'm sorry that I
worried you
this poem is a portrait
and a mirror
it's
"I'm okay"

(I'M SORRY)

This brain this day is scorpions,
    waiting
—like a vine-covered spike pit, waiting
—like a needle in a handful of rosary peas, waiting
—like a "Bless your heart"
    to leap,
    Unbidden, unrepentant,
from the unwilling den of my mouth

FIXING TO

Gather
    into the shaded spot that reminds us of our great grandmother's
hands
    she was
            is
    the sunny edge of the forest

It'll be hard to spin the dial
    deep:
flight paths & barking dogs and & creaking swings but
    there it is

    just below our narrative smirk, now fast
    we have only just enough time to be *so* genuine now

Crush the pokeberries between our fingers–
    (avoiding the nose & mouth)
Drop the dark purple mash into the inflatable kiddie pool, full up
    to the sea turtle rim with water & vinegar

& hope
    (the hope can be borrowed if we can't yet harvest our own)

wiggle our toes, through
    the water, in
    the berries, on
    the soft plastic, over
        sacred earth
drop each stitch to the unders and socks
    dipped wholecloth and naked under Her sun

    we might smell pipe tobacco
& hear
    the clatter of that old screen door

       .

—we were always exactly as the universe needs us
—quit your squallin'
—the biscuits need done
Our feet gone and dyed of the working, we won't go
barefoot for days, but—for at least a little while—
we're immune to our own poisons

KIDS THESE DAYS

Shades of green and gray
deep in that kudzu-covered mind
                    of mine
I can feel the Ancient Ones, wending
        through lobes layered thick with vine

and time.

I can sense them, poring over each
        tender
        blade of
        grass, each
            glimmer of june beetle, each

hope I hold loosely in my grasp
                    close.
their lips
        velvet-worn from long-familiar prayers
        whisper "wow,

I've never seen one quite like you before."

BRACKEN

Time doesn't require of us
    any
        single
            thing.

Press your body, into the yielding earth
Let your tongue do
as it might & touch
in the shady soil
spores
of the life you keep on not having
        left
           behind
It almost spins itself now: the dial to
    the feeling of sand slipping out beneath your toes

dryer buzz & door-to-door & have you heard the news & zero installation—
there
Cracked in the amber of that moment you don't talk about,
growing 360 million years from the trauma horizon of your event, a
    fern.

Light gets in.

Even so many intrusive things like a bit of summer sun.
It'll grow back.
You know that now, right?
Patch it with mantras&
        glitter&
        cocktails&
        performative vulnerability&
        tape
&
there's a couple ways you get out of this

You can spend the next three lifetimes waiting under moonlight for that
terrible moment
    to grant you a single pointless wish
Or, upon finding an old lighter that belongs
    to a limestone mold of a lesser you

set fire to frond
&hope for rain

the gleaning

What didn't you do to bury me
but you forgot that I was a seed.

—Dinos Christianopoulos

FOR SOMEONE WHO MIGHT—ONE DAY—BE YOU

rain, I pray, will bring bountiful your harvest
may it wash
(most) the grit that

could not cry away
leave you shining, new, birthed and
caught
by your own two hands

reach inside through fallow & fold
    blackberries
    honeysuckle
    volunteer tomatoes
    poke &
        dandelion fluff

& deep
    there it is

that sharp seed of glass, polished pearlescent
    transformed

by fire & flood & torrential time

& pluck

NOTES

"The One With the Cockroach" is inspired by two clearly superior poems: Nikki Giovanni's "Allowables." And Rudy Francisco's "Mercy."

"Good Vibrations" was inspired by a deep and brief dive into wondering if plants could hear. An article that I enjoyed on this topic: "Are The Plants Listening?" by Jon Lieff, MD, *https://jonlieffmd.com/blog/are-plants-listening*

"Thoughts &" was the winner of the 2023 Local Accents Poetry Contest hosted by Accents Publishing

"Bracken" first appeared in the *Yearling: Poetry Journal Volume 2* by Workhorse

"Trailhead of a Parallel World," "Good Vibes," "I am Reckoning with my Inheritance," and "Once Upon" all first appeared in *Etched Onyx Magazine.*

If you don't like the road you're walking, start paving another one.
— Dolly Parton

ACKNOWLEDGMENTS

This book is a process of unearthing the parts of myself that were failing to thrive and giving them a voice. Most of these pieces were written in the months leading up to my decision to quit consuming alcohol, the remainder written in early sobriety (sooner), then early widowhood (later).

Work like that doesn't pull neatly from the ground, and cannot be done alone. I am filled with infinite gratitude for my cohort of Katerina Stoykova's Poetry Book Bootcamp: Joanie DiMartino, Manny Grimaldi, Quincy McMichael, Glenna Meeks, Mary Elizabeth Moore, Lisa Miller, Bill Verble, and Jason Williams, and of course, Katerina herself. Every writer mentioned in this paragraph is a blindingly brilliant poet. Please seek out their words and allow them to transform you. Their counsel has certainly transformed me.

This will sound like a brag (and it is). The fierce and dedicated cohort of chosen family and family that has chosen me is too numerous to name, but know that I have felt your hands upon my back the whole time. I hope you've felt me, too. I've never been a person who has known how to feel like they deserve belonging, but that hasn't stopped you from caring deeply for me.

ABOUT THE AUTHOR

Renée Rigdon is a widowed, sober, nonbinary writer, artist, creativity instructor, and weirdo-about-town. They love blending the humor and tragedy of life into a milkshake of magic and hope. Their work reflects a deep connection to nature, the difficulties of being a human, and the aches and absurdities of everyday life.

In addition to poetry, Renée coauthored *The AntiCraft: Knitting, Beading, and Stitching for the Slightly Sinister* with the spectacularly talented Zabet Stewart.

When they are not writing, creating, or advocating for the importance of creativity for grown-ups, Renée fills their time with cat snuggles, jigsaw puzzles, and a good porch sit. They live in Lexington, Kentucky, with their awesome son and two absolutely precious perfect tortie cats.

Find Renée on *reneerigdon.com*.